Y0-CTS-694

Take a trip to
CUBA

Keith Lye
General Editor
Henry Pluckrose

Franklin Watts
London   New York   Sydney   Toronto

Facts about Cuba

Area:
114, 524 sq. km.
(44,218 sq. miles)

Population:
9,877,000

Capital:
Havana

Largest cities:
Havana (1,925,000)
Santiago de Cuba
(404,000)
Camagüey (262,000)
Santa Clara (189,000)

Official language:
Spanish

Religion:
Christianity

Main exports:
Sugar (about 80 per cent),
tobacco, fish, nickel

Currency:
Peso

Franklin Watts
12a Golden Square
London W1

Franklin Watts Inc.
387 Park Avenue South
New York, N.Y. 10016

ISBN: UK Edition 0 86313 498 X
ISBN: US Edition 0 531 10286 6
Library of Congress Catalog
Card No: 86 50896

© Franklin Watts Limited 1987

Maps: Susan Kinsey and Simon Roulestone
Design: Edward Kinsey
Stamps: Stanley Gibbons
Photographs: Paul Forrester 10; John Griffiths 8, 13, 21, 22, 23, 24, 26, 31; Network 3, 4, 7, 12, 14, 15, 17, 19, 20, 25, 27, 28, 29, 30; ZEFA 4, 6, 9, 16, 18:
Front Cover: John Griffiths
Back Cover: John Griffiths

Typeset by Ace Filmsetting Ltd
Frome, Somerset
Printed in Hong Kong

Cuba is the largest island country in the West Indies. It consists of one big island and more than 1,600 small ones. Cuba has much magnificent coastal scenery. It lies about 140 km (90 miles) south of Florida in the United States.

The explorer Christopher Columbus, sailing in Spanish ships, reached Cuba in 1492. He landed at Baracoa on the east coast. Columbus thought he had reached India and so he called the local people Indians. Spain took Cuba and Spaniards began to settle there in 1511.

The Spaniards set up large estates and forced the Indians to work on them. Many Indians died and, from 1517, African slaves were taken to Cuba to work the estates. The Spaniards built cities, such as Trinidad on the south coast. They ruled Cuba until 1898.

The United States defeated Spain in the Spanish–American War and ruled Cuba from 1898 to 1902. For many years American influence remained strong. American companies financed many businesses in Cuba's capital, Havana.

The old part of Havana contains the Presidential Palace, which is now a museum. This palace was the home of Cuba's dictator Fulgencio Batista, who fled in 1959 following a revolution led by a lawyer, Fidel Castro.

Cuba is a republic governed by the Communist Party of Cuba, the only party allowed in the country. A portrait of the President, Fidel Castro, is on the poster in this picture of a political rally in Revolutionary Square, Havana.

After the revolution, Cuba's relations with the United States became strained, and Cuba turned to Russia for help. But many Spanish traditions survive. For example, most people are Roman Catholics. The picture shows the Cathedral in Havana.

The picture shows some stamps and money used in Cuba. The main unit of currency is the peso, which is divided into 100 centavos.

10

WORLD MAP

Cuba

USA
Straits of Florida
Gulf of Mexico
BAHAMAS
Atlantic Ocean
Havana Matanzas
Cardenas
Santa Clara
Pinar del Rio Cienfuegos **CUBA**
Trinidad Camagüey
Isle of Youth
Holguin
Baracoa
Manzanillo
Santiago de Cuba
Guantánamo Bay
CAYMAN ISLANDS (British)
Caribbean Sea
JAMAICA
HAITI

11

This busy street is in Cuba's second largest city, Santiago de Cuba. This city in the southeast is an important seaport and it has many industries. It was founded in 1514.

Matanzas is a seaport about 100 km (62 miles) east of Havana. Founded in 1690, it serves a rich farming region. Seven out of every ten Cubans live in cities and towns.

13

Lowlands cover about three quarters of Cuba. Cuba lies in the tropics and so it has warm summers and mild winters. In most years there is plenty of rain. Because of its climate, Cuba has a generally green appearance.

The rainy season lasts from mid-May to October. The rain is heaviest in the highlands. The highest land is in the Sierra Maestra range. Fierce storms, called hurricanes, sometimes strike Cuba between August and October.

About 23 out of every 100 workers are employed on farms. Sugar cane is the most valuable crop and it accounts for 80 percent of Cuba's exports. Most of it is sold to Russia and other countries in Eastern Europe.

The cane is processed in sugar mills. Sugar processing is one of many industries in Cuba which make goods from farm products. With Brazil and India, Cuba is among the world's top three sugar producers.

Tobacco is Cuba's second most valuable crop. Tobacco and tobacco products, such as cigars, are exported. Other crops include bananas, coffee and cotton. Food crops include corn, rice and vegetables.

In recent years, the government has encouraged farmers to keep cattle on the rich pastures in the lowlands. Cuba now has more than five million cattle. Pigs, horses, sheep and goats are also reared.

The government owns about two thirds of Cuba's farmland. On co-operative farms, the farmers work together and share the profits. On state farms, the workers receive wages and do not share the profits.

Fishing is a major activity. The government owns a large fishing fleet. But many fishermen belong to fishing co-operatives, in which they work together and share the profits they make from their catches.

Cuba has some large forests and it exports timber and timber products. The timber in the picture has been cut to make charcoal. Such valuable woods as cedar and mahogany are made into furniture and other objects.

Industry employs 31 out of every 100 workers. Cuba's chief mineral is nickel. Many new factories have been started up recently, including this cement works. Other products include farm tools and fertilizers.

Education is free and compulsory for children between six and fourteen years of age. Cuban school-children get hot lunches free of charge. Free medical services have also helped to raise health standards.

About 70 percent of children of secondary school age attend school. Some secondary school children go on to one of Cuba's three universities— in Havana, Santiago de Cuba or Santa Clara.

Grandparents often care for their grandchildren during the day, because many mothers have jobs. Many Cubans, especially in the countryside, are poor, though living standards are steadily rising.

This family lives in a wooden house on a farming co-operative. In recent years, the government greatly increased health and other facilities in rural areas. Most districts now have primary schools.

Leading sports in Cuba include baseball, basketball and swimming. The picture shows a soccer match in progress on the Isle of Youth. This island, Cuba's second largest, was once called the Isle of Pines.

Cubans enjoy music and dance, which combine African and European styles. The rumba, mambo and cha-cha-cha are popular dances. Ballet, painting, sculpture and poetry are important art forms.

As in other Latin countries, carnivals provide the chance for everyone to have fun. The streets fill with floats, while dozens of bands play dance tunes. Carnivals in the cities also atract tourists and tourism is steadily increasing.

Many young Cubans belong to a youth organization called the Young Pioneers. They seek to keep alive the spirit of Cuba's revolution which brought Fidel Castro to power. They hope that by working together they will make life better for everyone.

Index

Arts 29

Baracoa 4
Batista, Fulgencio 7

Carnivals 30
Castro, Fidel 7–8
Cattle 19
Cement 23
Cigars 18
Climate 14–15
Coastline 3–4
Columbus, Christopher 4
Communist Party 8
Co-operatives 20–21, 27

Education 24–25

Family life 26–27
Farming 16–20
Fishing 21
Forestry 22

Government 8

Havana 6–9
History 4–7
Hurricanes 15

Industry 17, 23

Livestock 19

Matanzas 13
Money 10
Music 29–30

Presidential Palace 7

Religion 9
Revolutionary Square 8
Roman Catholics 9

Santiago de Cuba 12
Sierra Maestra 15
Spanish rule 4–5
Sports 28
Stamps 10
Sugar cane 16–17

Timber 22
Tobacco 18
Tourism 30
Trinidad 5

Universities 25

Young Pioneers 31
Youth, Isle of 28

JAMES PRENDERGAST

3 1880 0183230 4

J 972.91 L   c.1
Lye, Keith.
  Take a trip to Cuba
                      9.90

DATE DUE

JAMES PRENDERGAST
LIBRARY ASSOCIATION

JAMESTOWN, NEW YORK

Member Of

Chautauqua-Cattaraugus Library System